POEMS FROM
THE SAND

POEMS FROM THE SAND

STANCE FREEDOM

proving
press

Book Design & Production:
Columbus Publishing Lab
www.ColumbusPublishingLab.com

Copyright © 2021 by
Stance Freedom
LCCN: 2021905415

Paperback ISBN: 978-1-63337-489-8
E-Book ISBN: 978-1-63337-490-4

Printed in the United States of America
1 3 5 7 9 10 8 6 4 2

STANCEFREEDOM@MAIL.COM

FOREWORD

FIRST AND FOREMOST I would like to give a special thank you to the extraordinary wives of Chris Kyle and Shawn Thomas, two of my hero's. Without their stories I would have never been able to express my feelings toward our fallen brothers. I would also like to give a special thank you to all of our service women and men stationed all over this great planet of ours. Your Sacrifice is appreciated. One more special thank you to the countless fallen brothers and sisters past and present that have sacrificed everything to insure our way of life and future democracies around the world. Last but not least, to the readers of my book, without you this would have not even been possible.

It has been a struggle for me in this journey we call life. Fortunately and unfortunately I have learned more than I bear to acknowledge. I would also like to acknowledge a couple of beautiful friends of mine named Patricia and Cindy M., who's been there for me through some very dark times. My last acknowledgement goes to a special woman named Jessica who literally to this day means everything in the world to me. The nearly two years we were together was the happiest and most enjoyable time I have ever spent in my life. She is an amazing woman and an absolute joy to be around. She was also an inspiration for many of these poems. Without her presence in my life, I have no idea where I would be at this particular moment. She will always be in my heart and is certainly missed.

Some of these poems were written while down range in Afghanistan. Although I didn't encounter allot of which our brothers and sisters in arms did, I did encounter some. I would like to give tribute to all the men and women out there that sacrificed so much for this great country that I deeply love.

Throughout my life I have always wanted to write a book. Though I had no idea of a topic to write about, I have been writing poems on paper ever since I could remember. Sadly, many of those poems have been lost throughout time. I did however, write a poem for this book regarding the September 11th attacks. I wrote a similar poem back in 2001 right after the actual attacks took place and proceeded to fax it to the White House in care of George Bush. However, not surprisingly I heard nothing back. Unfortunately with all the other poems I wrote over time, that one was lost as well. It is only since June of 2011 when I deployed to Afghanistan that I started writing poetry again in my spare time. However, this time I decided to put these poems together for a book. I know it's been eight years of writing poems sporadically, but I will tell you that for me to write I must be inspired. As silly as it sounds, a couple of these poems I woke up in the dead of night just to write. I don't know what woke me up or gave me the idea to write but I am glad I did. Inspiration comes from the heart and mind working together.

Its November 30th, 2019 and these will be my final words I write for this book before I have it published. Through my life, I have endured a great deal of pain and emotional heartache. However, I don't think anything compares to the hurt I suffered the moment Jessica told me it was over. She is truly the only woman I can honestly say I loved with all of my heart. I am one of those few that believe in fairy tale love stories and true romantic blessings. No matter what happens, she will always be in my heart.

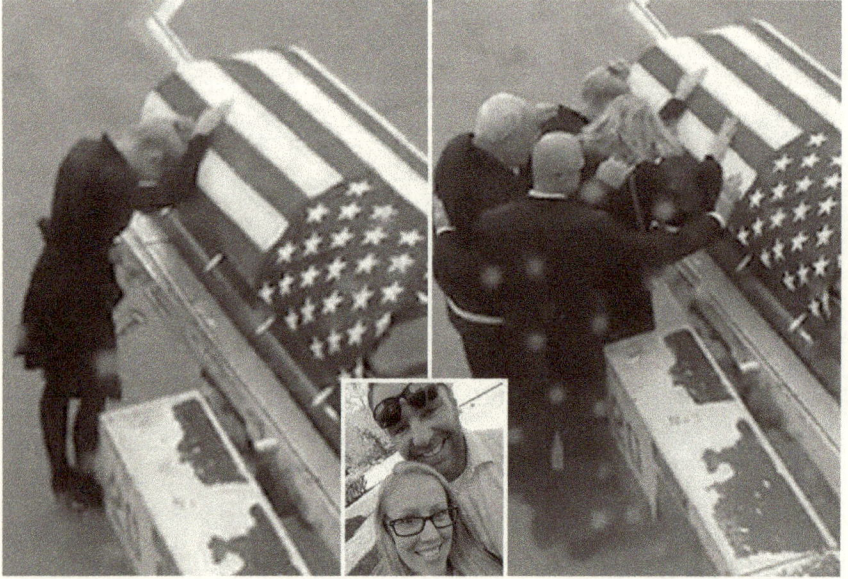

8 TOURS...

A true hero will journey
When the time finally arrives
Fighting for our nation
To save American lives

Traveling so far away
Leaving his family behind
As much as he loves them
He must clear his mind

Seven deployments
With this being number eight
As much pain as it would cause
God has chosen his fate

Back in the rear
His wife sobs at night
Trying So desperately
To keep tears out of sight

Unbeknownst to her
The pain would be to great
Seven trips overseas
His last is number eight

Notification of her loss
Would shatter her heart
The fragile pieces of her family
Suddenly missing a part

How does she tell her children
About the pain they will feel
They say time closes the wound
But it will never properly heal

The love of her life
Proceeds gently off the plane
She drapes over his coffin
Trying desperately to maintain

Uncontrollable tears
Is to much to bear
Her family walks over
And envelops her with care

My husband is home
No longer will he have to fight
I am confident That God
Has guided him to the light

Rest in Peace now Shawn
My one true love
Your are resting with the angels
In the heavens above

CHRIS...

Chris is a hero
With the sacrifice he would give
His countless acts of bravery,
Would ensure our troops would
live

Deep within the battles
He's the angel on overwatch
Ensuring that our missions
Would not end in botch

The atrocities Chris would
witness
From Al Qaeda's evil heart
Would test his humanity
But would not tear him apart

Im sure he wasn't proud
Of things he had to do
But defending this country
I know his heart was true

The best sniper in history
The military has said
Killing all the monsters
To avenge our precious dead

The sadness of this tale
Lies beyond his seal life
Retirement from that chapter
More time with his kids and wife

With all the days down range
And surviving all the death
The simplicity of civilian life
Would be his final breath

Killed by a former soldier
Who suffered PTSD
He took away our hero
And left us only the memory

As I write this with tears
Of another fallen soldier
I can't help but feel
The country is a little colder

For the heat from Chris's heart
Would keep us all warm at night
Because of his selfless service
And eagerness to do what's right

FLUID

Walking along the beach
I notice scenes of my life
Plagued with hardships
Shattered with strife

My heart was fragile
Open to a few
But my eyes were closed
My heart with no clue

Love is fluid
Like waves from an ocean
Subtle and smooth
With a sought out emotion

Love is an entity
That you must hold dear
For once it has you
Your heart will see clear

DAY 1

It's hot and I'm tired
The air is so dry
This tour's just begun
Am I too old to cry

I am a soldier
Crying is for the weak
Recognition and respect
Is what I aim to seek

The bombs and explosions
The chaos all around
My mind and my emotions
I try to keep sound

As the days get shorter
And the present becomes the past
The long plane ride back
I will be home at last

THROUGH THE CHILDS EYES

How do you explain the
reasoning
For the abuse of a child
Treated like an animal
Brought in from the wild

How do you construe
The marks left behind
A baby's tattered existence
In the hands of the unkind

The battering and belittlement
Each night and day
The unwarranted pain
The anguish and dismay

The innocence of a child's mind
Riddled with guilt
A subconscious wall of shame
Around him he has built

How much affliction
Should this child endure
How much pain
Before his heart is no longer pure

Acceptance is all he seeks
Compassion and the love
That was supposed to be
conveyed
From the heavens above

BREAST CANCER...

A survivor of fate
A hero to all
Gleaming with triumph
She heard the call

No fear in her heart
No pain in her eyes
She will face this affliction
No matter the size

With the long road ahead
Seeming so bleak
For its normalcy of life
She will ultimately seek

The suffering she has endured
Her soul in misery
She drops to her knees
Dear LORD why is it me

Why have I been chosen
For this unbearable task
Is it for the wrongs
I've committed in my past

My precious child
Light of my life
Chosen were you
To take on this strife

Not for my amusement
Nor your distress
It is your calling
'Tis simply a test

I have elected you
To lead the way
So others might follow
And not be led astray

You will show so many
That share your blight
You will show them your strength
And help them to fight

You will walk them through
sadness
And console them through
despair
You will hold them through the
bitterness
And show them you care

You are the one chosen
Your strength is your cure
For all you have helped
Know your heart is pure

LOVE LEFT BEHIND...

The sea is warm
Like the depth of my heart
Love drew us closer
Pain tore us apart

The last tear drops
The sadness will extend
The smile fades
The soul tries to amend

The days' drift by
With reflections of the past
The web of confusion
The stones we cast

The life we seek
The love we find
The affliction of our future
With the love left behind

WITHOUT...

Without peace
There is no calm
Without trust
There is no love

Without mistakes
There is no learning
Without pain
There is no sympathy

Without honor
There is no loyalty
Without truth
There is no honesty

Without submission
There is no eternal life
Without GOD
there can be no Forgiveness

GOD WILL NEVER...

A rose amongst weeds
Tree's surrounded by brush
A field of emerald grass
So beautiful and lush

The air so crisp
The water so calm
The prayers and teachings
From the word of PSALM

GOD is with us
This much I know
He's beside you in your highs
He carries you when you're low

Trust in him
To guide your way
For God will never
Lead you astray

ASHES TO...

Ashes to ashes
Dust to dust
Are we attracted to passion
Or hungered by lust

The world around us
Engulfed with need
A demand for pleasure
The pursuit a greed

We have turned to sin
To pave the road ahead
Scarcity of guilt
The life we have led

For many who have traveled
It's too late to turn away
Somewhere in the past
Morals went astray

Ashes to ashes
And dust to dust
Life is too short
It is GOD you must trust

MEND...

The soft kisses,
Her warm embrace,
Her sparkling eyes,
The smile on her face,

The sound of her voice,
The care in her heart,
The pain and anguish,
Being so far apart,

Praying this to be over,
So I can see her again,
Until that day comes,
My heart will not mend.

BREAST CANCER PART 2...

It shows no pity
And has no remorse
It will destroy
Throughout its course

Resilient it is
Powerful yet so meager
Waiting to ravage
With anticipated eager

It is not biased to ethnicity
Nor race or religion
Disfigure and kill
Is its isolated mission

It lurks in secrecy
Obscuring in its victim
Sometimes no clue
Not even a symptom

It exerts its wrath
From cell to cell
It's nothing short of evil
From the dark depths of hell

We must all unite
To weather the grief
Together we'll beat this
Is my infinite belief

So please join the struggle
We have all heard the call
Breast Cancer is horrific
But together we'll never Fall

911...

It was a warm sunny day
In this great country of ours
The trees were howling
The scent of the flowers

Little did we know
In the moments ahead
The towers would collapse
With 3000 dead

Our country held high
With freedom and pride
Suddenly attacked
By cowards who hide

We as a nation
Stood tall that day
All our petty differences
Temporarily swept away

We held hands and
prayed
We tightened our fist
with force
Our everyday lives
Were strewn off course

200 years of freedom
Suddenly seemed
fictitious
Because of the evil men
Whose intentions were so
malicious

Our soldiers stood up
To defend our great land
Men and women alike
Called hand in hand

A war on terrorism
The newspapers read
Eliminate the evil
To avenge our dead

Somewhere in war
Honor has its place
I'm afraid in this battle
Tis simply not the case

The terrorist exclaim
They do it for God
They say it's a holy war
They call it Jihad

I don't recall in the bible
That God said to kill
I do remember
That he gave us free will

These terrorists will have
you believe
That they are superior
That all non-Muslims
Are the ones who are
inferior

Men are created equal
I am positive the bible
reads
Eternal damnation
For those with evil deeds

18 years of war
With many lives lost
When does it end
And what is the cost

We are a nation of
freedoms
We are a nation of pride
To all the terrorists out
there
America will never run
and hide

PEACE...

The images of my past
Flood my mind
Reflections of the pain
Follow me from behind

Years of tragic guilt
Cry out in my soul
Life-long sorrow
That has blinded me whole

Sometimes my heart
Knew only hate
With a mixture of rage
That kept me up late

The boundaries are limitless
Its peace that I want
To sooth my spirit
So hate will no longer taunt

The difference then and now
Lies deep within me
Finally through the love
Is where I can see

MEDIC...

The goal for me as a medic,
Is to provide the best care
possible,
In a country that is unforgiving,
In a land inhospitable

The care is from my heart
Compassion from my soul
When all is said and done
War takes a toll

How many must die
To show the world we care
So many perished already
We must all look to prayer

The flag we hold high
The pride felt inside
The enemies will understand
America never runs to hide

We are a nation of freedom
We fought centuries to achieve
To the nations that aspire for
freedom
Your sides we will never leave

LOVE CEASED...

Death is not
What I fear the most
Poverty is what
I fear the least

What I fear
Can't compare
To a love that is fading
Or a love that is ceased

I miss her kisses
Her warm tight hugs
The hogging of the blanket
With those gentle little tugs

I miss her smile
Her soothing embrace
I miss her scent
The innocence of her face

I miss her eyes
And hope our hearts will mend
But most of all
Without a doubt
I miss my best friend

50...

Another day has arrived
Yesterday has passed
With her by my side
My futures bright at last

A gift was sent
From the heavens up above
An angel so beautiful
To shower me with love

Pain and hurt
Turned my heart cold
With her there to warm me
A love story will be told

The past has been rough
With nobody on my side
But the next 50 years
Will definitely turn the tide

With my Angel next to me
Deep inside my heart
For the next 50 years
I pray we are never apart

THE SIGN...

What does it take
To find true love
How often should you pray,
To the heavens above,

When is it time,
To know she's for you,
To thaw out your heart,
To prove she is true,

Where is the sign,
That will show us the way,
To enduring happiness,
Night after day,

Is GOD up there watching,
With sorrow in his heart,
Praying our path's,
Will not lead us apart,

Are there tears in his eyes,
From the road we chose to follow,
Where was the point,
When our souls became hollow,

Somewhere on this Earth,
Is the one we must find,
To shower us with beauty,
And a love that is to kind,

Somewhere beyond the horizon,
The one lies in wait,
The one GOD has chosen,
To be your soulmate,

There's only one chance,
To capture her heart,
To be blind to that chance,
Is to always be apart.

TWAS...

Twas the night before Christmas
When I heard a strange noise
Was it St Nick
With a sack full of toys

I crept down the stairs
With a joyful fright
What I saw
Was a painful sight

Mommy in tears
Sobbing by the tree
Thanking God for the miracle
The miracle that was me

I'm thankful for the love
My mom always had
Christmas without toys
Isn't so bad

For God took to my heart
And told me to pray
As he showered us with love
Night after day

ROSES ARE...

Roses are red
Clovers are green
At night I see your face
Deep in my dream

Long beautiful hair
Enchanting green eyes
Gorgeous smile
Like the prettiest of skies

I see her in the distance
Like a mirage in the heat
The scent of her perfume
To me is a treat

Kisses and hugs
From the depth of my soul
My heart used to be in pieces
But now it is made whole

SIMPLE...

It was just that simple
The love that was supposed to be
It was just that simple
A love that was so free

It was just that simple
Two roads intertwined
It was just that simple
A woman so kind

It was just that simple
Two hearts beat as one
It was just that simple
True love had just begun

It was just that simple
A woman so bliss
It was just that simple
A love sealed with a kiss

FOREVER...

Her eyes made of emerald
Her smile so bright
Kissing her lips
Holding her tight

Missing her daily
The warmth of her touch
Every day without her
Is a bit too much

Seeing her in my dreams
Yet so far apart
Waking up without her
Is a tear at my heart

Telling myself
We'll soon be together
Hoping the love
Will last forever

SENT...

Sent by angels
From the heavens above
The kindness of her heart
Was filled with love

Never in my days
I thought this could be
A beautiful woman
Who was sent to grace me

She has come into my life
To mend my heart
So it will never again
Be torn apart

I open my arms
With a warmth and love
Praying before God
That sits high up above

My dearest God
My voice echoed loud
Why have you sent me
This angel from a cloud

God Whispered back
In a nurturing voice
I opened opportunity
It was you that made the choice

Passing through the pain
To reach the other side
To open your heart
Where the love can reside

So revel in this moment
And embrace her love
For I will always lead you
From High up above

THE SUN HAS SET...

The sun has set
With a chill on my heart
My eyes start to weep
With us so far apart

Separated by distance
I stare up at the moon
Mesmerized by its light
Hoping very soon

As my heart grows fonder
For the woman of my prayer
I hope her heart is deep
Layer after layer

For the existence of love
Lies deep in my soul
For the woman of my dreams
Has again brought me whole

LONELINESS...

Loneliness is bitter
Like a cold frigid day
I stare at the heavens
On my knees as I pray

The tunnel is dark
Like the brilliance of night
The sadness creeps in
So tired of the fight

Sad thought instills us
Like bad memories in our mind
To hurt us or bewilder
Depression is unkind

A past full of madness
A world full of fear
The future unknown
My fate unclear

For one day soon
The grief shall be no more
Waiting for happiness
To finally fill my core

PRINCE CHARMING...

She lies in bed
Dreaming of a prince
A man that is charming
With no words to mince

Someone to love
Forever more
To cherish her ever being
Right down to her core

Ahead in the distance
The future is bright
Her destiny awaits
A glimpse of Mr. Right

Who can this be
Someone to call her love
A man that will carry her
Over mountains above

To nurture and support
Lend a shoulder if needed
To show her his love
Is very deep seeded

A man of her dreams
That God will surely send
Through his soothing grace
Her heart he will mend

FLOWERS FOR JESS...

Flowers for Jessica
The woman in my heart
So close in spirit
Yet so far apart

I see her in my dreams
On a warm pleasant day
She is my joy
In a world of dismay

Soaring through the heavens
With pain in my life
Searching for that special
someone
To call my wife

Looking through the past
I see a future that is bright
The ever presence of joy
Is clearly in sight

With the strength of her love
Deep in my soul
The whispers from her heart
Will soon make me whole

TO WHOM IT MAY CONCERN...

To whom it may concern
I give my life to thee
The passion in my heart
Is where I learn to see

The love I've lost
Through the passage of time
The love I've found
Will forever be mine

This poem I write
From me to you
Can only be said
From a heart that is true

From the moment I looked
Into those beautiful green eyes
I knew my sadness
Would turn to surprise

To hold you and kiss you
And never let go
You have comforted my soul
When my spirits were so low

To love and cherish you
To protect you with my life
I get down on one knee
And desire you as my wife

This I pledge
Till my dying day
I will love you forever
What else is there to say

LIGHTNING STRIKES...

Lightning strikes
Thunder claps
The bugle begins
As a soldier plays taps

Another hero gone
In a time of war
Pain in our hearts
Threaded to the core

When shall it end
All this death
The heart beat fades
He takes his last breath

The journey begins
His pain is no more
His soul is free
Amongst the heavens he will soar

Beside the Lord
He will remain
To finally be at peace
Once again

INTOXICATED...

Intoxicated by your love
Your dreams I will enter
My heart cradles the moment
Your kindness reaches my center

As the soul flourishes
With love from the earth
Ive been dreaming of you
Since the dawn of my birth

To hold you
To kiss you
To be with you forever
To walk with you
To run with you
Our love will not sever

The fluttering of the wings
From an alluring butterfly
Its elegance is overwhelming
Like the brilliance of the sky

As the night ends
And a new day has begun
From the settling of the moon
To the rising of the sun

Living my life
With you is my goal
For my love for you
Is the essence of my soul

SHE'S CRYING...

The flag is crying
Our country in despair
When will we wake up
And finally start to care

Poverty and homelessness
Have stricken our nation
It seems our humanity
Is on a permanent vacation

Declining education
The cost of our health
As so many greedy people
Increase their wealth

Companies going bankrupt
Welfare in full swing
It's taxpayers like us
Who definitely feel the sting

Employment on the decline
Unemployment on the rise
As our government continues
To burden us with lies

It's time for us as a people
To finally make a stand
Fixing our country
Is what we demand

So wake up Congress
And do something right
For the end of our nation
Is almost in sight

HAMPERED...

A soul filled with demons
Thorns in my side
How do I get away
Where to run and hide

A childhood strewn in chaos
Adulthood choked with loss
My sanity is in jeopardy
But what is the cost

Trying to survive
The only way I know possible
Did I stray off course
It seems very probable

Will the path open up
To a prosperous life
Will my mind that seems a blur
Finally gain its sight

Only time will tell
I hope it's not too late
For my heart is hampered
With anger and hate

GOD IS WATCHING...

The world is in chaos
All the violence within
The evilest of deeds
Humanity in sin

God has foresaw
The destruction we cause
To travel down this path
Will be a world without laws

We must live in peace
For the Bible is to preach
As our father in heaven
Will continue to teach

He has given us the ability
To live with free will
He has also explained
That thou shalt not kill

The most sacred of
commandments
Is what very few seem to cherish
Little do they know
Their souls will soon perish

I know my heart is pure
For in his hands I put my fate
My love for him is strong
No longer filled with hate

God is watching
Angry at the violence
If we do not change our ways
He will banish this world in
silence

MY GUIDING LIGHT...

Over the rainbow
Through the field
My heart did not stop
Did not even yield

The sound of your voice
The echo from your soul
My heart layered in ruins
Till you made it whole

Across the desert
Throughout the skies
I would travel the world
For a glimpse of those eyes

Through deadliest of storms
Or the cold dead of night
You are my true love
My guiding light

Hear my words
Listen to me speak
The one I have chosen
Tis you that I seek

From now until the end
I will love you forever
Forever as one
Eternally together

GREED...

So much greed
Spread across the land
So much violence
With the devil's helping hand

Why is it so
We need more and more
Is it the epitome of jealousy
Deep in our core

So many homeless
So many with needs
Is it too much to bear
To comfort with good deeds

So many rich
That do not share the wealth
So many poor
In such bad health

But God is watching
To those who are contrite
For he has a place for you
Within the light

For he who have greed
Deep in there soul
At the end of your road
You will definitely pay your toll

CARRY...

Together we were
Meant to be as one
To walk in the moonlight
And enjoy the sun

To live out our joy
To share our life
I as your husband
And you as my wife

Together we are
Meant to embrace love
To pray together
To the almighty above

Though I walk beside you
Holding you with pride
I will not hesitate to carry you
With all the love I feel inside

JESSICA...

Even though we're far apart
At no time will I tire
The passion I have for you
Will never cease to expire

My Deep caring feelings
And the joy in my heart
Wishing the time comes
When we're never apart

The nights are to short
And the days drag to long
Reminiscing your embrace
Keeps my emotions strong

Tis been awhile
Since I felt your touch
Jessica my beloved
I love you very much

Separated by horizon
Yet our souls are together
This much is true
I will love you forever

WHISPER...

To my God in heaven
I give my life to thee
Twas not forced
Or against my will
But done while I was free

I know you're up there
Whispering to my spirit
This I know for sure
For I can always hear it

You embrace my hand
And elevate my soul
Soaring through heavens
To make my spirit whole

The encouragement you give me
Is the strength that I need
I'll follow you anywhere
As long as you will lead

CAST...

As the rain sets in
I think of our love
Both come from
The heavens above

The rain seems pure
Like the joy in our hearts
As soon as we're together
Is when my life starts

As the rain gets harder
I gaze into my life
The mistakes I've made
Pierce my soul like a knife

The children I have
Relationships of the past
All would be tarnished
From stones I would cast

That time is gone
New days are here
The lives of my children
Are what I hold dear

I pray to my God
Please lead the way
Carry me in your arms
As I pray everyday

I heard his voice
Deep in my heart
My precious child
We've never been apart

Your troublesome days
And sleepless nights
I've always had you
Within my sights

Carrying and leading you
Through a world of strife
Only to guide you
To a better life

HERO'S OF THE PAST...

Martin Luther King
JFK
Struggled for human rights
Night after day

Both great men
Cut down it their prime
Praised through history
Honored throughout time

Rosa Parks refuse
To sit in the back
Pride and determination
She did not lack

Heroic Harriet Tubman
Ushered the way
To a path to freedom
From slavery everyday

Lincoln freed slaves
For the good of all man
Struck down with hatred
By a Confederate hand

So many great people
Fighting for equality
Only to suffer
The present days futility

Racial turmoil
Has encompassed us with hate
But hatred for different races
Is certainly not innate

So many have perished
To give us our rights
The path to our happiness
Is with in our sights

The gangs and the violence
That plague our youth
Seems racially motivated
And that is the truth

We as a nation
Must get over this hate
Before we are judged
At heavens gate

For God has no pity
For those who do harm
It's time for your soul
To ring its moral alarm

HUMANITY...

The thoughts I have
And memories I hold
Have chilled me to the core
Like an icy winter cold

God walks beside me
And looks over me from above
But in my most troublesome
moments
Is when he carries me with love

Flowers bloom
In the spring time with joy
The amazing smile
Of a sweet little boy

Birds chirping
In harmony with pride
With peace and love
Spreads kindness from inside

The oceans are calm
At a blissful pace
The anger and violence
Amongst the human race

When will this world
See the beauty within
To start learning to live
Without the negativity of sin

Only when we see
The purity of God's heart
We can live in peace
Without being so far apart

JESSICA...

The days are long
Nights are short
Two ships that pass
With no site of port

Longing for your smile
And your soft tender kiss
I look to the sky
It is your heart that I miss

I gaze at the horizon
And search for her love
I plead to the heavens
My lord from above

Tis the woman of my dreams
The one I wish to hold
To warm my soul
Instead of being cold

Jessica my love
I think of you ever day
I miss you so much
What else is there to say

Soon I will see you
And hold you with my heart
And pray on my knees
That we will never be apart

Stance Freedom

12-16...

December 16th
A day I won't forget
The beauty of the night
While the sun will soon set

She entered my life
And joy gripped my heart
Was the beginning of something
wonderful
My happiness would finally start

Her eyes sparkled
Like emeralds in the mist
Until it finally happened
The moment we kissed

The night felt to short
But the passion was there
Such a gorgeous face
With long silky hair

She invited me to her house
To continue our night of fun
Hoping it would last
Until the morning sun

Sitting on the couch
We sat hand in hand
Kissing her passionately

My heart would demand

She led me to her room
Anticipation of making love
Can this be her
My angel from above

After passionate love making
We cuddled about
But then all of a sudden
She kicked me the hell out

It was a playful little kick
As we kissed goodnight
The very next day
I was on a flight

Heading back to Texas
With her in my heart
Planning the move to Las Vegas
Where a new chapter would start

Three months later
We would finally be together
Praying to God
It would last forever

43

CANDLELIGHT...

Candlelight and quiche
Pleasure to the taste
A love between strangers
Is not such a waste

Candles and a bubble bath
Soft sensual kissing
Without you in my life
Something would be missing

Dinner I would make
For you every night
Candlelight and quiche
With you in my sight

Love flows through me
Like waves on the ocean
A smile from your lips
My heart filled with emotion

Together we are
The love that will be
Our hearts mend as one
Forever and eternally

Candlelight and quiche
For you my love
For you are my angel
From the heavens above

HERE LIES...

Here lies thy spirit
Spread beautifully in the cloud
Here lies thy soul
Growing large and very proud

Here lies thy heart
Beating and filled with love
Here lies thy joy
From the heavens above

Here lie our lives
Together as one
Lying in the light
Under a beautifully lit sun

Blanketed by warmth
I gaze into her soul
For in the midst of my heart
There once was a hole

Our eyes meet
Like lovers in the night
Losing you my love
Comes as a tearful fright

For you are the one
That lights up in my heart
For in my dreams
We are never apart

THE CURE...

Walking along the beach
The sun lit sands
Opening my life
To the warmth of God's hands

I pleaded with him
To show me the way
Living with the guilt
Night after day

Hoping this life
That is plagued with hate
Will soon know the truth
And be guided to a pure slate

The sin of man
Is to dreaded to bare
A world of anger
With no love to share

The violence and conflict
All over this earth
The innocence of a child
We care for at birth

When does this child
Begin to know fear
To feel the pain
But shed no tear

Why doesn't love
Enter their heart
Instead of the hate
Ripping it apart

We can only pray
To the God that is pure
And realize his forgiveness
Is the only cure

ONE DAY...

Gaze into my eyes
Take my heart in your hand
Walking into eternity
Making love in the sand

Racing the wind
Moving the moon
Together forever
One day soon

Caressing my soul
With your enchanting green eyes
A love that is forever
With a bind that ties

Deep within my sleep
Dreaming of you
Loss of control
With a love that is true

Not a day goes by
When you're not in my thought
The kindness and joy
Tis you I have sought

Let us be together
Through pain and despair
For I will be not beside you
But holding you with care

My dearest love
The joy for my heart
Let us never again
Be so far apart

TIME...

Tis hard enough
To meet the right girl
To follow your dreams
For the love to unfurl

From a place of solace
We ride the winds
Through the sands of time
We let go of our sins

The moon tells a story
As we walk in the sand
Gazing at the beauty
Walking hand in hand

The beginning of our life
The journey has begun
Contemplating our existence
With the setting of the sun

Can this be true
Do hearts really weep
For the love you find
Is the love you keep

The end of our journey
We shall know true love
From the girl that was sent
From the heavens above

SAILING THE WINDS...

Sailing the winds
With an open heart
So many miles
Us torn apart

Riding the clouds
Through the light of the moon
One-day sweetheart
One day soon

Your eyes glisten
Like diamonds in the ocean
A heart shedding tears
Filled with emotion

I've traveled the path
That leads up to your soul
You've filled my life
And again made me whole

To live without you
Is to never know love
To never feel joy
From high up above

My dearest Jessica
Love of my life
You have brought me from a
world
That was tattered with strife

So now I shall thank you
Everyday we're together
For now is the beginning
For us forever

FREEDOM...

Fighting for our country
With the flag in our heart
Separated by countries
So far apart

We fight for freedom
The terrorists we seek
The blood of our enemies
Will surely leak

Foreign or domestic
We do not care
For those who try to harm
Their lives we'll not spare

Like the veterans before us
Who gave all they could
Before our nation
Is where they stood

To defend it proudly
Before the flag they stand tall
All gave some
And some gave all

So cherish the memories
And be thankful of soldier's pride
For our country's men and women
Will never run and hide

DOMESTIC VIOLENCE...

She lies on the cold floor
Battered and bruised
Wiping away her tears
As she seems confused

With reflections of false guilt
Her emotions run deep
Curled up in a ball
As she continues to weep

Out of the corner of her eyes
Glancing down the hall
The sight of her little boy
Made her yearn to crawl

With her abuser hovering
And brandishing a hateful grin
It was though he was inhuman
Undaunted by sin

As she reaches her precious son
And embraces him with concern
This evil monsters hatred
Again starts to churn

She begs and pleads with him
To spare their child from grief
To postpone the continued abuse
If only for a brief

As the coward deviates
And heads the other way
She settles her baby to bed
And begins her long pray

As exhaustion sets in
But with God in her heart
She furiously begins to sob
Appealing for a fresh start

God clutches her soul
And whispers in her ear
The strength you possess
Will help you see clear

Rise up through the ashes
And journey beside me
For there is light through the
tunnel
And soon you'll be free

BLURRED...

As I look at my hardships
That has caused me great strain
An angel suddenly appears
To alleviate my pain

The laughs we had
The joy you brought
Happiness with you
Is all that I sought

Where did I go wrong
What has occurred
For my eyes are not blind
But my heart is now blurred

So once again
The storm appears
The spillage from my heart
In the form of hard tears

I walk now in silence
A piece missing from my soul
For in my shattered existence
Emerges an enormous hole

As the future may hold
What will forever be
The one that I love
Will forever hold the key

CASTING...

Casting my shadow
The pain is intense
The loss of your love
Is enormously immense

Walking in time
At an eternal pace
Joy and happiness
A never-ending chase

The sky is crisp
Not a cloud nor a breeze
The benefits of life
Are what I'm here to seize

The pain and sorrow
Are Chill to the bone
The emptiness inside
Has stranded me alone

Sooner or later
The pain will end
Tis only then
Will my heart start to mend

THE END...

Day by day
Night after night
The love slowly fades
With no end in sight

The pain of the loss
Is to much to bear
Why doesn't she love me
Why doesn't she care

For the beginning was bliss
Happiness foretold
But the end came near
With the heart turning cold

Passing each other
Like two ships in the ocean
Glancing at each other
With the absence of emotion

Was it meant to be
Was this supposed to last
I guess we'll never know
For its all In the past

So good bye my love
You'll always be In my heart
Certain pieces of my life
You will always be a part

LEGACY...

The air is warm
The sea is cold
Dreams are forgotten
But the legacy is told

Drifting through life
Like drifting through the ocean
The stress is relentless
The pent up emotion

Searching for our reason
Looking for our cause
Glorifying life
Taking a moment to pause

Why are we here
This gift we are given
What motivates our heart
To keep us driven

Do not fear death
Fear life without love
And remember God is waiting
In the heavens above

MOMMA...

My dearest momma
Joy of our heart
Even though you're in heaven
We're never far apart

In life your spirit
Flowed through us with love
Now it flows free
In the heavens above

You taught us respect
You taught us to forgive
You taught us to love
And taught us how to live

Next to God you are
With your husband beside you
God will comfort you both
This I'm sure is true

So rest now momma
For now you're at peace
Our love for you
Will never cease

GODS LOVE...

Walk in the sunlight
With the shadows behind
Erase all the anger
And live to be kind

Hate is a path
That leads you astray
It doesn't heal the heart
But leaves it in decay

The bitterness of the past
Leads the wrong direction
Seek to the Lord
For his protection

You must understand
That the root of all evil
Begins with the devil
And your soul's upheaval

Do not let him in
For Satan is weak
God is the love
You should be willing to seek

SIN CITY...

She walked into my life
With a gorgeous little grin
A diamond in the rough
Amongst a city full of sin

Her eyes made me smile
The joy in my heart
An angel in my life
She now is a part

In a time of trouble
My happiness seemed bleak
Laughter and joy
Is all I would seek

Tears In my eyes
From the pain I've been through
But now I have hope
All because of you

FRIENDS FOREVER...

Friends forever
incased in your love
You pushed at my heart
With a forceful little shove

The days go by
With no end in sight
Looking to the future
with a strong will to fight

friends forever
hoping we will be
Blinded by happiness
But yet able to see

my soul was in chaos
when you were not here
Twas shrouded in darkness
But now has become clear

A clouded existence
Used to lie ahead
Before we finally met
It was my future I most dread

friends forever
Patti and I will be
but without your friendship
I can never be free

XMAS...

Tis the season
For joyous love
Christmas was given
From the heavens above

A caring heart
Spreading gifts and cheer
The reason for family
Is certainly clear

From the center of our mind
Through the depths of our soul
Love is the soothing ointment
That keeps our heart whole

So on this blessed day
Let it be known
That the fabric of our being
Has already been sewn

PERSISTENCE...

In the face of betrayal
The midst of a shattered heart
The warmth of your soul
Guided a fresh start

The heartache and pain
That plagued my existence
It had no mercy
But showed its persistence

Through the end of the tunnel
Appeared a bright light
Her beauty and aroma
Twas a beautiful sight

The warmth of her skin
The glistening of her eyes
She wiped away the tears
And whispered no more cries

The beauty of her smile
The depth of her soul
Grasped at my heart
And proceeded to make it whole

For it will take some time
For the pain to subside
But with her in my life
There is nothing more to hide

TRUE LOVE...

Standing on the beach
With you in my arms
Gazing in your eyes
Seducing you with my charms

Nestling closer
To feel your warm skin
A night without you
Would be my only sin

As the gentle night nears
While the sun will soon set
I thank the lord
For the first day we met

As the days trickle by
And the years become past
I have found my true love
My true love at last

NEW LIFE...

I ask for a new life
I pray for a new dream
Wishful thinking is what I have
Or though it would seem

I carry myself on
Dredging through this existence
Respecting the challenges
Admiring the persistence

The lack of my confidence
My guilt in despair
Remorse without thought
My feelings I don't share

My voice echoed loudly
Each word expressed with hate
The long road ahead
Is blackened with no fate

Cursed on my birth
Failures lie ahead
A path to misery
To which I've been led

The days will go by
As time slips away
A life filled with misery
But yet I still pray

WOUNDED HEART...

A wounded heart
Stays quiet in the dark
Twas my task to be silent
For my soul to hark

The still of the night
Creeps gently through my mind
My emotionless glare
Struggles to be kind

Standing alone
Amongst the trees
Feeling the emptiness
Of the love he never sees

The path that once was
Leading to the light
Has strayed of course
With no end in site

I kneel to the earth
For my guilt ran deep
Giving my heart
For the lord to keep

I heard the voice
From somewhere up above
Whispering softly
Gentle words of love

For now I know
That God is my keeper
His love for mankind
Can not get any deeper

MINCE...

Words that you mince
Send shock waves through my soul
My grief from your actions
Has taken its toll

The story I tell
From a year that has passed
Hoping life with you
Would certainly last

Then came the call
Heartache on the other side
Giving you my attention
For you to confide

The sorrow through your voice
Echoed words of despair
Though love was not to be
You expressed you'd always care

As my soul started to fade
And the tears began to flow
I pleaded with her to stay
I begged her not to go

The words that you minced
On that fateful last day
Suddenly became clear
And left my heart in decay

DEPRESSION...

Another day of somber
Another night passed
Fatigue sets in
With depression that was cast

My eyes are drifting
Toward eternal night
My soul is lost
With no rest in site

The light I once saw
Fades into black
The love I once felt
Is now what I lack

The joy that I crave
The happiness I seek
Seems to decline
And never to peak

I finally drift away
On a nightmare with no end
For some it seems rare
For me it's a trend

Dreaming through the night
Of a love that'll never be
Like floating on an ocean
With no land I can see

Morning has arrived
The day starts out new
Unfortunately for me
There is still nothing new

REMORSE...

The story goes
The sea has no remorse
Sailing through eternity
And strewn off course

Waves upon waves
The power and might
The harder we fail
The brighter our sight

It is incumbent on our souls
For us not to quit
You must try your best
For the candle to stay lit

Through your eyes and your heart
You must work to succeed
Either follow a righteous path
Or by all means take the lead

Life isn't hard
Like you choose to see
Your strength lies in wait
For you to be free

DATING APP...

As I lay here at rest
Remembering the love lost
I ask myself why
While calculating the cost

From the instant I found her
On a popular dating app
Twas the moment of truth
I could never go back

My heart skipped a beat
For hours we would talk
I knew the moment we met
Our eyes would certainly lock

Drinks would start our night
Dinner would come after
Joy filled the air
From both of our laughter

Playing pool was our next venture
It was either hit or miss
Half a game played
I reached in for a kiss

The softness of her lips
Sent warmth through my soul
Is this the young lady
That would make my heart whole

The night finally ended
The air filled with bliss
We walked to her car
Again another kiss

I pleaded with her to stay
Begged her not to go
Eventually she drove home
With me in tow

Couple hours at her house
We called it a night
Seeing her again soon
Would be such a delight

As I drove away slow,
Thoughts of love sprinkled the air,
Seems like I found a woman,
That would finally care.

HER EYES...

Her eyes glistened
Like diamonds in the light
The smile she wore
Was a delightful sight

The elegance of her voice
As she whispered to my heart
I knew when I met her
My true happiness would start

Gentle kisses every night
Hugs during the day
Love throughout an eternity
what else is left to say

This beaten path through life
Has left me in sorrow
But with the future looking
bright
There will always be tomorrow

Relishing her appearance
Gazing deep into her soul
She has gripped my heart
And finally made it whole

As we journey together
And discover a joyous life
The greatest gift I could want
Is calling you wife

Until that day happens
It's a blessing with you near
I pray that we stay together
Year after year

CLOSER...

My heart was frightened
Closed from despair
An emptiness throughout me
Humanity didn't care

Searching for a reason
To keep my spirit whole
Praying on my knees
Through the depths of my soul

Out of the light
A faint little shine
The sight of an angel
Hoping she'd be mine

It was though she was floating
Through the air with such bliss
Praying for the chance
Of an intimate little kiss

Closer and closer
I anticipated her touch
Never realizing In the future
I would care for her so much

Finally face to face
I was lost in her eyes
Never again to be sad
And definitely no more cries

She's entered my soul
She's tugged at my heart
A bright new beginning
With a fresh new start

A beautiful angel
Has emerged in my life
To fill me with joy
And relieve me of strife

So thank you my love
For my dreams have come true
Our friendship is forever
And I will always love you

FREEDOM...

Our government wants us to
believe
That we are free
Two hundred years have passed
Yet I still can't see

The eagle is sobbing
At the pain we endure
For government is a disease
And we have no cure

Taxes are ridiculous
Unemployment is in full stride
With members of Congress
Running to hide

The borders are open
For anyone to cross
Free medical to illegals
But what is the cost

Let's not forget to mention
The terrorists at hand
Causing violence and chaos
Across our great land

Our veterans are homeless
Hungry and sick
Does our government give a dam,
Or is the money to quick

The world looks at us
As a nation of envy
The truth will illustrate
That we are ultimately free

Government will lie to your face
And say they mean well
What I say to them
You can all go to hell

CHILDREN...

Children are a blessing
Cherish them well
For the eyes of your loves
Will surely cast a spell

Nowhere does it say
You can't spoil them rotten
Somewhere along the road
People have forgotten

Educate your children
For discipline is the key
Show them respect
And through their heart they
will see

Manners are a must
Show them the way
Thank you and your welcome
Teach them what to say

Even when it's time to punish
Common sense should be sought
Eagerness to be harsh
Should never be taught

Treating your kids
With the love they deserve
Will certainly ensure
Your relationship will preserve

So in my closing
I would like to say
Always love your children
For forever and a day

WIFE...

I see her face
Across the room
Her smile opens up
Like roses that bloom

I gently walk toward her
With thoughts of a kiss
Will I score
Or will I shoot and miss

Carefully she turns
With a grin on those lips
Only to reveal
Those beautiful hips

Closer and closer
I start to stare
With no thoughts of anyone
Not even a care

Finally it happens
She looks at me intense
The emotions run deep
So deep they're immense

Our lips draw near
With a soft sensual touch
The woman of my dreams
Whom I love so much

Thankful she's blessed
My heart with her life
Hopeful she will continue
To forever be my wife

EARTH IS DYING...

Earth is dying
At the sin of man
They say we can't fix it
Our future demands we can

Trash in the ocean
Our sea life in despair
Is your conscience blocked
To not even care

Pollution all around
Temperature on the rise
Is it global warming
Or all a mass of lies

The reality is this
Money is the cause
To many hypocrites
With to many flaws

No longer can we afford
Our selfish way of life
For the future of our children
Will certainly bear the strife

We must work together
For this vicious cycle to cease
So future children will live
With some form of peace

Our earth is dying
At the sin of man
Instead of turning a cheek
Let's lend a helping hand

FDA...

Orange's, apples
Bananas, and pears
Does anyone eat them
Who the hell cares

Cauliflower and broccoli
Carrots and peas
Good for the body
So give me seconds please

Ice cream, popsicles
Pie and cake
But not until after
Baked potato and steak

Peanut butter and jelly
Turkey and ham
Not as disgusting
As that garbage called spam

Nuts and berries
Whole oats and grains
Black and red licorice
And yummy candy canes

What does this poem mean
Since I wrote it so fast
Eat what you want
The FDA can kiss your ass

BEAUTY ALL AROUND...

Waves flow through the ocean
Like wind through the trees
Birds glide through the air
With the greatest of ease

A bear and her cubs
Nestled close for the night
Sun setting in the distance
Tis a beautiful sight

A wolf teaching her young ones
How to hunt and track
Looking up to mom
As the leader of their pack

From the furriest of rabbits
To the gentleness of fawn
Beauty is all around us
In our hearts we are drawn

Why is it that man
Chooses to ravage
Is it unintentional
Or do we enjoy being savage

Whatever the reason
Our future we should address
Humanity needs to realize
Our planet is in distress

If the world strikes back
For our irresponsible ways
It will be tomorrow's children
Who certainly pays

WIFE PART 2...

From the birth of a child
To the death of man
The hourglass runs
Filled with sand

Take one step at a time
For life can be sweet
Experience all you can
Because everyday is a treat

Find your soulmate
And smother them with love
Pray everyday
To the heavens above

Walk hand in hand
With joy in your heart
Knowing your love
Is not far apart

For when the day comes
To depart this life
Your soul mate was your best friend
To whom you called wife

ETERNALLY...

The warmth of your body
Your skin next to mine
Sitting in front of a fire
With a nice glass of wine

Looking into your eyes
Kissing those sweet lips
The caressing of my hands
Against those soft sensual hips

As I slide inside you
With love in my heart
Nothing on this earth
Could pull us apart

The excitement is building
As I whisper your name
The animal inside us
Cannot be tamed

Our fluids are flowing
Without hesitation
Being inside you
With a loving sensation

Closer and closer
The feeling is bliss
The climax begins
As we romantically kiss

As I lay on top of you
I look into your eyes
My endless love for you
Is of no surprise

To my darling sweetheart
Love of my life
I'm eternally grateful
That you are my wife

WAR...

War is hell
It has been said
With so many lost
And one to many dead

Why is there such conflict
Between all of man
Why can't we just talk
With peace in our hand

The violence and terror
That strikes at our will
Our lives are what evil
Seeks out to kill

Blood fills the streets
Cries heard in the distance
We must not underestimate
Evils persistence

God has enabled us
The choice of free will
He has continuously warned us
Thou shalt not kill

We should all heed the knowledge
And change our ways
So that we may live in peace
The rest of our days

SCHOOL...

Blessed by thy school
Thy tree of knowledge
One more day
Before I start college

Knowledge and truth
Is my goal to achieve
Ambition and fortitude
Have forced me to believe

The road has been long
The journey has been hard
The memories of the past
Have definitely been scarred

Forks in the roads
Obstacles in the way
Have left my life
In deep disarray

That time is over
A new life has began
For now and through the future
I will always believe I can

VETERAN...

The military veteran
A survivor of hope
His wounds from the wars
He must learn to cope

WWII to Vietnam
Iraq to Afghanistan
To the ordinary citizen
They will never understand

Hours upon hours
Guarding a wall
Just to insure
There is safety for all

The flag still waves
Our soldier's stand tall
For when it's time to defend
Our men and women heard the call

So let's give thanks
To all our nation's vets
And pray that our country
Never forgets

YOUR CHOICE...

To those who strive
Failure is not a choice
To those who give it all
They triumph and rejoice

Their sweat and their pain
The anguish and the tears
Have not been for nothing
Nor wasted years

The strength within your soul
Is delaying its clout
Extending its dormancy
Waiting to burst out

So for all of those
Who strive for perfection
Search your soul
For your own reflection

VOW...

My vow is sacred
The love has been shared
Throughout my life
Thy self has not cared

Wanting and waiting
Looking for my soul
Waiting for my mate
To again make me whole

Forever is her beauty
An angel from design
Through her beating heart
I'm given a sign

Blessed be my heart
Since she's walked in my life
The only thing remaining
Is for her to be my wife

JUNE 9TH...

June 9th
The day of her birth
I am honored and privileged
She has graced this earth

Walking through the sunlight
Her warmth and her glow
The love from her soul
She will soon bestow

Never have I encountered
Such beauty and delight
To see her in my dreams
Is a glorious sight

I thank you my darling
From me to you
For my love for us
Will forever remain true

YOUR HAND...

Twas the night before your birthday
And all through the land
Down on one knee
I asked for your hand

Praying for the response
To be gentle and kind
Not no but yes
Was running through my mind

A hug we will share
Followed by a kiss
To be lost in your eyes
I will certainly reminisce

Growing in age
Together for all time
The bells of love
Will certainly chime

Love is forever
My love for thee
Even in heaven
Will last eternally

ACCIDENT...

Once in a great while,
You cross paths with a radiant
light,
An undeniable shining star,
Who's future is so bright,

Intelligent and strong willed,
She refused to soften,
Advancing toward her dreams,
As she did quite often,

With her arduous ambitions,
Her goals within sight,
Her world would soon crumble,
Extinguishing that bright light,
The accident that was caused,

In that picturesque little town,
Would unravel so many lives,
And turn them upside down,
The crash that seemed small,

That happened in a moments
breath,
Soon would turn grievous,
With the result of her death,
Again a bright light,

Would light up her way,

For her life was no more,
God asked her to stay,
Although she felt peace,

And the love was so immense,
The taking of her life,
To God made no sense,
Again with his love,

He guided her way,
She awoke from death,
This time to stay,
But the road that lie ahead,

Was strewn with debris,
Even though she was awake,
It was hard for her to see,
So began her recovery,

With family at her side,
The pain she would go through,
Was impossible for her to hide,
Relearning to walk and talk,

Doing it all over again,
But just as important,
Was teaching her heart to mend,
For two years after this tragedy,

He obviously had no heart,
Her fiancee up and left,
And wanted no part,

Little did he care,
Of the extra pain he would cause,
Her determination was
unstoppable,
And would never be put on
pause,

This young lady is progressing,
But has a long road to go,
With all the love in her corner,
She has plenty of room to grow,

So to this beautiful woman,
This radiant bright light,
New dreams are ahead,
So never give up the fight.

OSAMA...

If you look up in history
The evils of man
One comes to mind
That plagued our great land

Bin laden was his name
A coward without emotion
Hiding in a cave
Across a great ocean

Little did he know
America in it's glory
Would gear up to strike back
And put an end to his story

Afghanistan and Iraq
Pakistan to name a few
The elite of our soldiers
Were determined to pursue

Through the blistering day
And the cold dead of night
The man who was gutless
Would remain out of sight

Although he had terrorists
To guard him at all cost
He must have been scared
That his life would soon be lost

Arriving in the dead of night
Two helicopters cross the border
Training for this very moment
They were finally given the order

Landing in the courtyard
Would be a complicated chore
One chopper had crashed
And had shaken them to the core

But our seal team was resilient
Putting their fear in the back
Stone cold bravery
They certainly didn't lack

Entering the building
The clock began to tick
Finding this monster
Must be done quick

As civilians around the
compound
Ventured from their sleep
The thought of being
compromised
Would slowly start to creep

Maneuvering through the rooms

With stealth and speed
Taking out his son
Up the stairs they proceed

9 minutes has elapsed
As they reach the third floor
They observe bin laden standing
Through a wide open door

With a weapon at his side
Danger was in sight
The team Was very focused
And ready for a fight

But without taking a chance
The seals raised their M4
Killing bin laden
Dropping him to the floor

Heading downstairs
With bin laden in tow
They placed him in a bag
With a proverbial red bow

Gathering intel
Including bin laden's journal
His atrocities in history
Will unfortunately remain eternal

A 40 minute mission
Almost flawless from the start
It's only a needle prick
But straight through Al Qaeda's
heart

This heinous man is dead
Thrown into the ocean
It is difficult to show pity
Or the slightest of emotion

This man was evil
Down to his empty soul
His legacy of death
In the form of human toll

But our country will prevail
As we did in wars past
Our enemies will always perish
But America will forever last

MY HEART WILL SHINE...

Though we've never met
I can sense the delight
For sadness endured
Until you hit my sight

Searching this world
For a second true love
God took the first one
But gave me another from above

An angel has fallen
To grace my life
Lord knows my pain
And senses my strife

Words we would share
Nights full of conversation
Never would I have thought
You would be my salvation

The heartache of losing love
Is to great to bear
All I really sought
Is someone who would care

Your beautiful brown eyes
Extraordinarily kind heart
Even though we've never met
It's certainly a beautiful start

I foresee a glorious future
With you on my arm
You cherishing my soul
As I shield you from harm

Day trips for pleasure
Nights that are too short
I will seek out your spirit
For its you I want to court

So the days carry on
And the love will forever grow
The illustration of my happiness
From all aspects will show

As this monologue begins to close
And my words come to an end
The gratitude I have
To you I will send

Until we first meet
And the love starts to chime
Tis only then and there
When my heart starts to shine

THE YOUTH...

Today's day and age
The youth lacks respect
They think violence is the answer
In fact that's incorrect

It is something you earn
With a kind gesture and smile
Not something you practice
With error and trial

The definition of respect
In the dictionary is clear
Nowhere does it say hate
Or even to smear

But that's what people do
In today's new age
It's time for the world
To start a new page

Respect should be in our heart
From the day of our birth
Not just in our nation
But all over the earth

So many of our youth
Lack the knowledge they seek
The teachings from home
Today's parenting skills are weak

Parents blame a busy world
But an education is just
To teach your children respect
Is not just your job but also must

Along with respect
Is knowing wrong from what is
right
Learning to deal with problems
Is not to far from sight

You as the parents
Must teach your youth
The differences of lies
And the God's honest truth

Until that day rises
And you take control till the end
The lack of respect
Will continue to be a trend

NP...

N-P has risen
To the levels of disgust
Her once beautiful city
Is nothing short of a bust

Sanctuary is its motto
With criminals and their behavior
This once glorious destination
Desperately needs a savior

In comes POTUS
To try and stop the devastation
But liberals oppose it
As they take tax payer vacation

Opening the borders
Is what she demands
Destruction of America
Is in her evil plans

Free medicare for all
Along with school tuition
As illegals invade this country
And try to ruin this great
institution

But real Americans say no
To breaking this great nation
Standing up for the constitution
Is our only salvation

So to all law abiding citizens
I implore you to stand up
And tell all the liberals
To shut the hell up

EW...

E-W claimed to be native
1-1000th was the ultimate fact
Pocahontas would be outraged
At her sheer lack of tact

Far from Native American
Unlike Irish blood in my veins
Her character and her
truthfulness
Is littered with tattered stains

She claimed to be Cherokee
With a DNA test she took
Native Americans rose up
And slapped her on a hook

The stance she had taken
Had caused quite a stir
It's apparent that her common
sense
Was an absolute blur

Now she's up and running
For the 2020 bid
Prancing around the country
Like a confused little kid

So many controversies
Involved she has been
Now she agrees with socialism
And it's become a scary trend

She calls the wall immoral
And legal Americans are unkind
But what she doesn't realize
Is her stupidity has made her
blind

She's blind to the fact
That our resources will not last
If we open up for everyone
They will certainly run out fast

So in this closing rant
I encourage you to write a letter
And close our dam border
And focus to make our country
better

IMPEACHMENT...

Democrats have succeeded
Impeachment has begun
A circle of total lies
The leftists have spun

With the house run by dems
Ukraine is the new adventure
The truth and the real story
Is what they hope to censure

Seems Biden was the culprit
His son involved to
But dems chose to ignore
The foot with the other shoe

The facts seem clear
The truth shall be revealed
If the libs have their way
The evidence would be sealed

All the libtards want
Is trump's head and nothing more
Power and greed is what they seek
Right down the their very core

We as Americans
Must open our eyes
Do our own research
And expose all their lies

But until we step up
And start using our brain
The culture of their stupidity
Will be a permanent stain

WE AMERICANS

The ordinary citizen
Most powerful entity on earth
Not for the last few years
But from the dawn of everyone's
birth

Why are we as a consumer
Not taking a stand
The government doesn't own this
country,
American's own this land,

Everyone is tired
Of the politically correct word
Grow some thick skin
Because it's getting absurd

If you wanna make a change
Send Congress a choice
Do the right thing
Or we will raise our voice

If the loud voice doesn't work
I suggest a call to action
Treat Congress and its cohorts
Like a corrupt evil faction

Your money and your time
Is how this country works
Cut it off for one day
Knees will buckle from all these
jerks

Send a letter to Congress
Explaining your stance
Pledge one specific day
And everyone take a chance

When this day reaches
Boycott your life
Stay home from everything
You and your wife

Don't go to work
Nor to the store
Don't go anywhere
Punish them to the core

Hurt them in their pocket
The source of all evil
Make them all quiver
With corporate upheaval

The American people,
Are the true power in this nation
Once you realize your strength
It is a wonderful sensation

We as a world
Must stand up to the corrupt
Or continued abuse of power
Will always be abrupt

300,000...

300,000 victims
Does that number suffice
All those poor children
Harbored like mice

Used for sexual pleasure
Sodomized and raped
Your evil mind goes further
And decides it should be taped

As you climb on top
The victim whose 16 years old
Raping her defenseless body
As her soul turns brutally cold

Just remember karma
It could be your daughter
Thrown to the wolves
As sexual fodder

Children are exploited
In this country everyday
Where is the humanity
Why is it in decay

The purity of these children
Horribly stripped from their core
Never again able to love
From their heart has been tore

The innocence has left
From the actions of many
Politicians do nothing
Which is not uncanny

But the people are getting tired
Of your thought and no action
When a child is trafficked
By a disgusting mob faction

WOUNDED...

As I sit at the VA
Looking at a wounded soldier
I can only imagine
His heart growing colder

The bitterness inside
At the injuries from war
Eating at his heart
Stabbing at his core

As he sits there in silence
Remembering the battles fought
The lesson he takes with him
Is a hard lesson taught

His battle buddies have passed
Only to be dearly missed
60 years have gone by
From the time he would enlist

That time's come and gone
The sacrifice he would bear
Do the people know his suffering
Do they really even care

Waiting for our doctors
I walk up with a sense of pride
We were in different wars
But we were both on the same
side

Even though I am a veteran
There is simply no excuse
If you don't appreciate past
veterans
You are nothing but obtuse

WATERS...

Dirty waters are flowing
Through the cess pool of LA
For a useless politician
It's just a normal day

The streets littered with garbage
Drug use in full swing
It doesn't affect her
Society will feel the sting

Now it's on to finance
My God in heaven
She's clueless on budgeting
She couldn't run a 7-11

But she's in control
Of our nation's wealth
She's obviously an idiot
Running under a mode of stealth

Push back on Republicans
She ignorantly said
For her hatred for Americans
Her true colors have been shed

Common sense she lacks
And dumb as piece of lint
But blind to this fact
She doesn't get the hint

She calls us deplorable
She should first look at her city
It's the definition of deplorable
Its nothing less than shitty

So wake up America
And see the idiot for what she's
worth
A mistake to our country
A real deplorable to planet Earth

NOT MY PRESIDENT...

Not my President
Is what they choose to yell
Socialism and banning the 2nd
Is the argument they try to sell

1st amendment on the block
No longer does your voice matter
Democrats and left liberals
Sound more like the mad hatter

College and Universities
Operated by the Dems
Rhetoric and bias chaos
Is where it all stems

The truth and its history
No longer plays a part
The brutality of their actions
Have galvanized their heart

Antifa and all its violence
Strewn across the land
Spewing all the hatred
Aligned with the devils hand

Where does this all end
The lunacy of their action
As the days go on
They sound more like a corrupt
faction

We the people
In all it's robust glory
Should stand up against
ignorance
So we may tell a better story

About this great nation
And how we overcame
The demagogues and the corrupt
To truthfully place blame

In my closing of these words
Let us not forget
That we fight for this country
And should never feel regret

VALUES...

The heart of this country,
Eroding from the core,
Values and principles injured,
Like a wide open sore,

The depth of our constitution,
Shredded and cast,
Turmoil in our present,
From the sins of our past,

The poison of racism,
Still ravages our society,
While certain leaders of this land,
Clash for notoriety,

In truth these grandstanders,
Care nothing of you and me,
Power and greed,
The only appointment they see,

Words that are spun,
And perverted for their gain
Media with their twisted facts,
Can make anyone go insane,

Does the truth even matter,
Or do your feelings take heed,
The blatancy of ignorance,
Has planted its seed,

Your self entitlement and self
indulgence,
We've grown irritable and
disturbed,
The thought of your contribution,
Has us all rather perturbed,

For the youth of today,
Common sense has been lost,
The destruction of our country,
Unfortunately will bear the cost,

I call on Americans,
To open your dam eyes,
To research who's truthful,
And who spreads these evil lies.

NOVEMBER 23...

November 23rd,
2015,
The first day of interaction,
I could never have foreseen,

The next couple of years,
Such happiness and bliss,
With December 16th,
Commencing with small kiss,

It was a dream come true,
Phone texts kept climbing,
24 thousand and counting,
Its what I call perfect timing,

Anticipating a lifetime,
Of happiness and glee,
All because of Jess,
Giving her heart to me,

Is there a definition,
For the elusive word perfect,
In my eyes it was her,
Yes Jessica was perfect,

From lunches to dinners,
To shopping for clothes,
To rubbing her feet at night,
Even her cute little toes,

Weekends of joy,
Laughter at the pool,
Relaxing at Mt Charleston,
Where the air was crisp and cool,

As I sit hear in tears,
I miss her with all my heart,
Praying for the fairy tale,
With a big missing part,

Maybe someday,
When my heart starts to mend,
Life will guide us,
Together again.

HOLLYWOOD...

As untouchable as he is,
He is easy to analyze,
He hates Trump with a passion,
As he stands on stage and cries,

Uttering "F" "U" Trump,
Are the words from his mouth,
While illegal immigrants,
Pour in from the south,

The raging bull is angry,
One of acting's killer elites,
As gang members and illegals,
Take over Cali's streets,

Entertainer's call him a legend,
A good fella by his friends,
But the ignorance from his words,
Hatred is all he sends,

From the mean streets of New
York,
To Florida across the US,
Whenever he opens his mouth,
There's nothing but a pool of cess,

Wishing he feels the heat,
Is the mission I continue to
pursue,
This so called man of honor,
Is anything but true,

Once upon a time in America,
The President felt respect,
But the grudge match between
politicians,
Has the country feeling the affect,

As I bang the drum slowly,
And put a conclusion to this
plight,
If he wants to punch someone in
the face,
I'm ready for his gutless fight,

So from a man who's not a fan,
Who would like to be an advisor,
Take your obvious lunacy,
And become a taxi driver.

MAGA...

This is MAGA country,
With a noose around his neck,
Little did the country know,
He had already written a check,

With his acting mediocre,
To the police he reported a crime,
It was all a made up hoax,
Which is severe this day and time,

A week before he cried wolf,
A threatening letter was received,
Little did we know,
The country had been deceived,

Charges filed by the police,
Against this obvious nobody,
The evidence overwhelming,
As everyone could plainly see,

More obtuse disregard for law,
Would soon follow suit,
A Chicago DA dropped all
charges,
Apparently trying to look cute,

Racism definitely played a part,
But reversed it may have seemed,
To spark his failing career,

The media wisely deemed,

Court records ordered sealed,
So the public would never know,
The damage was already done,
This idiot fired from the show,

The records have been unsealed,
A new judge has commanded,
Investigations now at hand,
The truth has been demanded,

So now were all in need,
For justice to level its scale,
Hopefully this con artist,
Will most certainly go to jail.

CORRUPT TO THE CORE...

Happiness filled the air,
In the year of '82,
The world was advancing,
For both me and you,

Little did she know,
That a recording would be taped,
The scandals would just begin,
The cover-ups would soon be
draped,

Laughing at the thought,
Of a rapist being let off,
He passed on a polygraph,
As she let out a cheerful scoff,

Knowing he was guilty,
She laughed about the fact,
You wonder where the justice
was,
Or even simple tact,

The next several years,
Would see a cluster of deliberate
debacles,
While good politicians in this
country,
Evaded a slew of obstacles,

Watergate to Travelgate,
Even the infamous Emailgate,
The gates have certainly opened,
But prison life is not to late,

All through the 90's,
Turbulence filled the "House",
Anyone leaving this place,
Should certainly delouse,

Back door deals and inside
agreements,
To this day still exists,
Financing and cooperation,
Will harbor the terrorists,

Then came Benghazi,
And all the ludicrous lies,
Washington was a pile of feces,
Swarming with diseased flies,

With all the false reporting,
From the "Man" in the "House",
And his crusty sidekick,
With the see through blouse,

They informed our great country,
That Benghazi was in no trouble,
Apparently those two imbecile's,
Are happy in their little bubble,

No boots on the ground,
Was the "Man" and his sidekicks
position,
Obviously to dim-witted,
To realize a future inquisition

The report finally published,
From the Benghazi select
committee,
But the two grungy rats,
Did not feel the slightest of pity,

Four Americans were slaughtered,
On September 11th of all days,
But the American people,
For bravery gave them praise,

The sidekick went on her way,
To challenge the "Man" for his
spot,
But again the emailgate returned,
And once more she was caught,

Lying seems to be her motto,
The core principle of her soul,
In the grand scheme of life
though,
She's nothing but a little troll,

To end this little story,
She needs to be in a cell,
After she's finished there,
I'll be relieved when she's in hell.

DREW...

Since the first time i saw you,
As a cutie in ET,
Being nearly the same age,
My heart still fell for thee,

Fire starter was another,
As she was building her fame,
Her movies and her acting,
Would make her a household
name,

It was not until my early 20's,
That i would eventually come
clean,
Drew was my number one,
Not only in my dream,

My 30's saw peak maturity,
And bragging over her beauty,
Not just because she's gorgeous,
But she's just an outright cutie,

Seeing her on covergirl,
Certainly hit the heart,
She is absolutely breathtaking,
But I'm sure that's only one part,

40's have been great,
Her birthday 3 days from mine,
Part of me writing this book,
Is to carefully throw her a sign,

My favorite movie without a
doubt,
Might surprise you all,
50 first dates takes the cake,
Now just waiting for the call,

Ha ha a call from Drew,
Have you lost your mind,
Why would Venus goddess of
love,
Go out of her way to be kind,

As stunning as she is,
Sexy and so much more,
She understands the little people,
And the pain felt throughout
your core,

In closing of this plea,
My words are far from hollow,
Stay a little cutie Drew,
The sexiness will always follow.

KNOCKING ON THE GATES...

Knocking on the gates,
Praying I'm let in,
For I've tried my best,
To avoid evil sin,

I know I'm not perfect,
And I have made many mistakes,
I've tried to do what's right,
Whatever it takes,

From the day of my birth,
To my teenage years,
There has been plenty of sorrow,
And a steady flow of tears,

My 20's finally arrive,
The problems did not sway,
Mistakes plagued my life,
Troubles did not go away,

Although my life,
Would certainly move ahead,
The thought of being a father,
Is what i most dread,

Then my children were born,
And my emotions set in,
My beautiful children,
Made me forget all my sin,

My 30's saw me commit,
Too the service of my country,
It finally became clear,

My responsibilities and duty,

9 years in the service,
I don't regret at all,
What hurts me the most,
Is seeing our soldiers fall,

50 is almost here,
It's hard to fathom that age,
Most of my early life,
Was spent in a mental cage,

Now that I'm free,
Mistakes are far in between,
I look back on the past,
And wish i could've foreseen,

Where i would be now,
And what i have done,
Everyday is a new,
With the rising of the sun,

One day will come,
When i will not wake,
I beg for forgiveness,
For the love of God's sake,

Knocking on the gates,
Hoping to be let in,
Praying that God,
Will forgive me of my sin

HOLLYWOOD REMIX...

Hollywood California,
Home of the stars,
Fancy restaurants,
And million dollar cars,

Where everyone is corrupt,
Especially democrats,
The lowest form of life,
The little filthy rats,

Open the borders,
Let everybody in,
All races and nationalities,
And even their kin,

Some point in the future,
The balloon will certainly burst,
It seems our great land,
Has most definitely been cursed,

Criminals and drug dealers,
Just stroll over the border,
Bringing their poison,
No regards to law and order,

The wall Trump is building,
Is one tool for success,
We need more border patrol,
We certainly don't need less,

Now it's defund the police,
As ludicrous as it sounds,
MS13's murderous thugs,
Are populating our towns,

Where are the liberals,
And democrats of DC,
Flying on private jets,
And raping the money tree,

George and his losers,
Of the proclaimed blm,
Care less about people,
Than the money they skim,

Little do they know,
Their time is running thin,
For the strength of our country,
Will prevail us in the end.

SILENCE...

All these poems,
You have read in silence,
I appreciate you generosity,
Your love and your kindness,

Without the readers,
My book would not be,
Hoping these readings,
Will open your heart to see,

All of the chaos,
And turmoil on this earth,
To the moment we die,
From the moment of birth,

Hoping and praying,
We all come together,
To make it a better place,
Now and forever,

I'd also like to thank,
My family and friends,
With them in my corner,
My heart never descends,

And to the amazing Jessica,
Who has graced my soul,
Without her in my life,
I could never be whole,

To finalize this poem,
Let me just say,
God is watching over,
So let us all pray.

www.ingramcontent.com/pod-product-compliance
Lightning Source LLC
La Vergne TN
LVHW011210080426
835508LV00007B/701